INLET ISLES
A Hospital Foodservice
Case Study

Amy Allen-Chabot, Ph.D., R.D.

Anne Arundel Community College

Suzanne Curtis, Ph.D., R.D.

University of Maryland

Alma Blake, Ph.D., R.D.

University of Maryland

Prentice
Hall

Upper Saddle River, New Jersey 07458

Library of Congress Cataloging-in-Publication Data

Allen-Chabot, Amy.
  Inlet Isles: a hospital foodservice case study / Amy Allen-Chabot, Suzanne Curtis,
  Alma Blake.
     p. cm.
  Includes biographical references.
  ISBN 0-13-032836-7
     1. Health facilities—Food services.   2. Health facilities—Food
services—Management—Case studies.   3. Hospitals—Food services—Management—Case
studies.   I. Curtis, Suzanne, Ph.D.   II. Blake, Alma, Ph.D.   III. Title.

  RA975.5.D5 A43 2002
  362.1′76—dc21
                                                                    00-051048

Executive Editor: Vernon R. Anthony
Production Editor: Marianne Hutchinson (Pine Tree Composition)
Production Liaison: Barbara Marttine Cappuccio
Director of Production and Manufacturing: Bruce Johnson
Managing Editor: Mary Carnis
Manufacturing Manager: Ed O'Dougherty
Art Director: Marianne Frasco
Cover Design Coordinator: Miguel Ortiz
Cover Design: Joe Sengotta
Marketing Manager: Ryan DeGrote
Editorial Assistant: Susan Kegler
Interior Design and Composition: Pine Tree Composition
Printing and Binding: Victor Graphics

Prentice-Hall International (UK) Limited, London
Prentice-Hall of Australia Pty. Limited, Sydney
Prentice-Hall Canada Inc., Toronto
Prentice-Hall Hispanoamericana, S.A., Mexico
Prentice-Hall of India Private Limited, New Delhi
Prentice-Hall of Japan, Inc., Tokyo
Pearson Education Asia Pte. Ltd., Singapore
Editoria Prentice-Hall do Brasil, Ltda., Rio De Janeiro

Prentice
Hall

10 9 8 7 6
ISBN 0-13-032836-7

CONTENTS

INTRODUCTION

The purpose of this case study is to give students a chance to apply what they have learned in foodservice operations and management to a complex "real-life" situation. Specifically, students will have an opportunity to look at a food service operation in detail and perform evaluation, problem solving, financial, staffing, and planning functions. The case study includes a narrative about the foodservice operation, an organizational chart, staffing information, budget and weekly operating report information, menus, and problems or activities.

A computer disk with the weekly operating report and master schedule form is also included so students can practice making employee schedules and assess how changes in expenses or revenues influence cost per patient day.

This case can be used in its entirety or in partial form, depending on how it fits into a syllabus or course outline. It can also serve as a foundation for additional problems and activities designed by the instructor or supervised practice program director.

We hope that this case study workbook will provide an opportunity for applied learning, critical thinking, and fun for students and instructors alike.

The references below may be useful for gaining a better understanding of the principles illustrated in this case. More specifically, the book *Measure It, Manage It* can provide a more detailed step-by-step guide to understanding the financial reports. In addition, the text *Food for Fifty* contains most of the recipes listed on the menus. The other textbooks, *Foodservice Organizations: A Managerial and Systems Approach, Health Care Food Service Management, Introduction to Foodservice* and *Management Practice in Dietetics* provide a comprehensive overview of foodservice management and operations.

References That May Be Helpful in Completing Case

Richards, L. (1997). *Measure It, Manage It*. Chicago, IL: The American Dietetic Association.

Molt, M. (2001). *Food for Fifty*. (11th ed.). Upper Saddle River, NJ: Prentice Hall.

Spears, M. (1995). *Foodservice Organizations: A Managerial and Systems Approach* (3rd ed.). Englewood Cliffs, NJ: Prentice Hall.

Sullivan, C., & Atlas, C. (1997). *Health Care Food Service Systems Management.* Gaithersburg, MD: Aspen Publishers.

Payne-Palacio, J., & Theis, M. (2001). *Introduction to Foodservice* (9th ed.). Upper Saddle River, NJ: Prentice Hall.

Hudson, N. (2000). *Management Practice in Dietetics.* Belmont, CA: Wadsworth Publishing.

Amy Allen-Chabot
Suzanne Curtis
Alma Blake

CASE NARRATIVE

Inlet Isles Medical Center is a 375-bed private hospital located in the heart of North Miami Beach, Florida. The facility runs at approximately 75 percent occupancy but can drop as low as 50 percent occupancy in the summer and can exceed 100 percent occupancy during the heart of the winter season. The hospital is a general medical/surgical facility with a neuropsychiatric ward and a relatively large outpatient kidney dialysis center. The average patient age is 72 years and Jewish by ethnicity, but the orthopedic physicians do admit younger clientele on a regular basis. The hospital has been operational for thirty-two years but is in some financial crisis now due to shorter patient stays and reimbursement by diagnosis related groupings (DRGs). This Medicare reimbursement system tends to favor younger patients who can recuperate from medical interventions and illnesses much more quickly. Staff at the hospital totals 1,245 and includes many allied health professionals, environmental services employees, and administrative employees.

The purpose of the Department of Food and Nutrition Services (DFN) is as follows:

- To prepare and serve meals to patients in accordance with high sanitation standards, departmental budget allocations, and physician orders.
- To provide appetizing meals to personnel in a pleasant and enjoyable environment.
- To provide meals and snacks for specialized functions as requested by the administration.
- To provide clinical nutrition consultation and education as needed for both inpatients and outpatients.

To this end, the department provides services to inpatients, outpatients, employees, and visitors through the efforts of 58.5 full-time equivalents, which includes a management team of six full-time individuals. The organizational chart for the department is attached. Alicia Deerborne, the foodservice director, is responsible for all aspects of the operation and completes all the financial reports herself. She represents the department on hospital-wide committees and also oversees her two assistant directors. Alicia is aware of the financial crunch that the hospital is experiencing and her goal for the upcoming year is to reduce expenses and increase revenues. Jack Perry is the assistant director in charge of cafeteria, purchasing, and production. He comes to the position with considerable restaurant experience and enjoys the more regular and predictable hours that hospital foodservice offers. Nancy Newbury is the chief dietitian and assistant director in charge of patient services. Her areas of responsibility include the diet office, trayline, hostesses, and clinical dietitians. She is an experienced dietitian and has considerable energy and a very cooperative attitude. The employees sense that she cares and actually seem to help her to succeed. At present there are three full-time dietitians, but this area is targeted for reductions. Margo covers general medical floors, which include a predominance of endocrinology and gastroenterology cases. Cancer patients are also found in considerable numbers on these floors. Patrick covers the cardiovascular center and cardiovascular floors. He deals almost exclusively with post–myocardial infarction patients and bypass patients. Shirley covers nutrition support and the critical and surgical care units. She also covers the outpatient renal dialysis unit.

The department uses a conventional production system for all its meals, and the majority of food is made in-house. Convenience foods are purchased from Baxter Foods for special diets, as needed. Foods are prepared, held hot or cold, and served as quickly after preparation as possible. In addition to cafeteria and patient services, substantial finger food is being requested by the dialysis center and the on-site daycare center.

**Food and Nutrition Services
Organizational Chart**

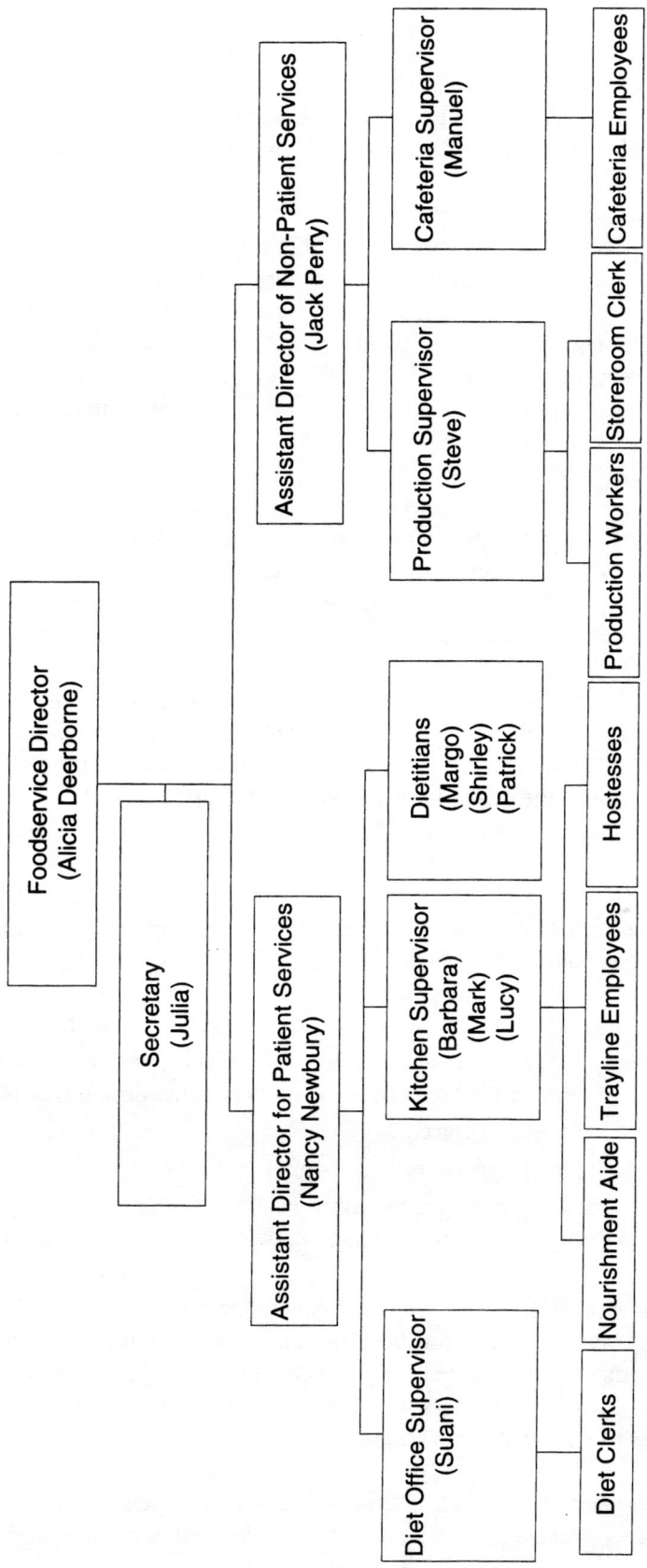

```
                    Foodservice Director
                    (Alicia Deerborne)
                           |
                    Secretary
                    (Julia)
                           |
          +----------------+----------------+
          |                                 |
Assistant Director for             Assistant Director of Non-Patient
Patient Services                   Services
(Nancy Newbury)                    (Jack Perry)
          |                                 |
    +-----+-----+-----+            +--------+--------+
    |           |     |            |                 |
Diet Office  Kitchen  Dietitians  Production     Cafeteria
Supervisor   Supervisor (Margo)   Supervisor     Supervisor
(Suani)      (Barbara)  (Shirley) (Steve)        (Manuel)
             (Mark)     (Patrick)
             (Lucy)
    |           |                  |                 |
  +-+-+     +---+---+          +----+----+           |
  |   |     |       |          |         |           |
Diet  Nourishment  Trayline  Hostesses Production  Storeroom  Cafeteria
Clerks Aide        Employees           Workers     Clerk      Employees
```

Patient Service

Diet orders are written in the charts by physicians or nurses via physicians' instructions. Diet orders are then sent to the diet office by the unit secretary, using the computer system. Diet office clerks then update the diet information and add or adjust a menu as needed for the patient.

A seven-day selective cycle menu is in place with menus for regular diets as well as calorie-controlled, sodium-controlled, fat-controlled, soft/bland/low-residue, renal, pureed, and clear/full liquids. Patients on other diets receive the menu that most closely relates to their diet and items are added or crossed off as necessary to meet the patient's diet prescription. Menus for the following day are delivered to patients with their breakfast meal. A volunteer then comes around to each room in the middle of the morning, collects the menus, and gives them to the diet office personnel. The only patients who do not receive a selective menu are those on pureed diets and clear or full liquids. This represents approximately 8 percent of patients.

The percentage of marked menus (where patients have actually marked the menu with their selections) is presently approximately 46 percent. Frequently, when patients fill out their daily menu, they write in foods that they want if they don't see the foods on the menu. Alicia sometimes wonders why she sends printed menus up at all since the patients seem to feel that they can request any food that they can dream up! Whenever possible, the department tries to honor special requests.

Prior to service, all menus are reviewed and marked menus are corrected in accordance with the patient's diet. Thus, if the patient marked something that he or she was not allowed to have, that item was taken off the menu and/or another item was substituted, if appropriate. Immediately prior to meal service, menus are checked against the computer list to assure that all diets (and NPO orders—no food by mouth orders) are correctly noted. Menus are then brought out to the trayline and meals are assembled in their usual fashion.

The trayline has six positions with the supervisor routinely responsible for checking trays for accuracy. Trayline positions are as follows:

Position 1: Puts menu and then tray on conveyor belt and adds diet packet and condiments.
Position 2: Puts cold salads and desserts on trays. Salads are kept refrigerated until time of service but are held at room temperature during trayline operation.
Position 3: Plates hot entrees.
Position 4: Plates vegetables and soup.
Position 5: Adds beverages to trays.
Position 6: Checks trays for accuracy and puts on lid.

The trayline runs at approximately 1.7 trays per minute for the breakfast and lunch trayline (full-time employees) and 2.9 trays per minute for the evening trayline (part-time evening crew). Based on supervisor assessment, it was noted that Lucy runs the trayline significantly faster than Mark or Barbara. Currently, Barbara works the morning shift, Mark works the evening shift, and Lucy is the relief supervisor (replaces Mark and Barbara on their days off).

Foods are organized in the steam table based on panning charts for each meal. A taste and temperature panel is conducted immediately prior to each meal to be sure products meet standards in

4

terms of quality and temperature. Nancy Newbury, one cook, and the kitchen supervisor participate in the taste and temperature panel. Products are generally heated if they do not meet temperature standards. If the item does not meet quality standards, a decision is made at that time regarding whether to serve the item or pull it and substitute something else.

Once the trayline begins, it is often necessary to stop the trayline in order to get special items that patients have written on their menus or for the checker to call for a missing item. The tray system used in this operation is an insulated tray from the Therma-tray company. Trays are able to hold food at a given temperature for 30 minutes or more before temperature loss occurs. The trays were purchased from Therma-tray nine years ago and are definitely beginning to show their age. The trays are generally easy to work with, but occasionally a patient orders more food than can fit in the compartmentalized tray. In this case, some food is deliberately left off unless the patient is on a high calorie/high protein diet. In that case, two trays are sent to the patient so all the food can be provided.

After a tray is checked by the checker, the lid is placed on the tray and it is placed in specially designed carts, which are steam cleaned once a month. When the cart is full, a hostess will take the cart to the appropriate floor and deliver the trays accordingly. Hostesses use an elevator, which is specially designated for dietary during the meal service. However, many people ignore the special designation and hostesses often have to wait for an elevator to arrive. Each hostess works four 10-hour days with an unpaid lunch and dinner break of 30 minutes each. Thus hostesses are able to deliver breakfast, lunch, and dinner on a shift of 7:30 AM to 6:30 PM. The hostesses find this draining, but enjoy the three-day weekend. Hostesses are trained to greet each patient cordially and verify the identity of the patient verbally or by checking the label on the bed. They leave the tray on the patient's bed stand but are instructed not to touch or move the patient in any way. When time permits, hostesses are instructed to check back with patients to see if they have everything they need.

Tray accuracy audits are conducted regularly by sending "dummy" trays to floors. In this instance, a dietitian will mark a menu and label it with a fictitious patient's name and include the room number of an empty room. The dietitian will then send it through the trayline as if it were a real patient tray and take it off the cart for evaluation when it reaches the floors. The dietitian then evaluates the tray to see if the items on the tray are correct according to the menu and that the temperatures are appropriate and appearance is good. Recently, temperatures for hot food have ranged from about 90 to 100 degrees Fahrenheit and cold food temperatures have ranged around 55 to 60 degrees Fahrenheit. The appearance of the tray is quite good and accuracy is approximately 72 percent with higher inaccuracies at lunch and dinner than at breakfast.

Cafeteria

The cafeteria is operated for three meals each day for both employees and visitors with a schedule of operation as follows:

Breakfast: 6:30 AM–10:00 AM
Lunch: 11:30 AM–1:30 PM
Dinner: 4:30 PM–7:00 PM

The menu used for patients is also used for the cafeteria (7-day cycle menu), but a daily special is offered in the cafeteria to reduce monotony. A theme day with special items is planned once per month.

5

The cafeteria can get quite crowded during the peak of service and lines can stretch into the causeway outside. Dietary employees are responsible for keeping the cafeteria clean during the meal time but Environmental Services does a major overall cleaning each evening. The positions allocated to the cafeteria include two servers for each meal with one cashier for breakfast and dinner and two cashiers for lunch. The cafeteria supervisor also circulates during the meal service, handling problems and concerns as they arise. Temperatures of food on the line in the cafeteria are consistently appropriate and servers are pleasant although reserved. Every attempt is made to keep the dining room stocked during service with trays, silverware, napkins, and so on, but often supplies will run low during peak times. The customer base for the cafeteria is 65 percent hospital employees and 35 percent visitors. Average total meal count at breakfast is 175 with a meal count of 650 for lunch and 350 for dinner.

Menu prices in the cafeteria tend to be calculated by doubling the food cost for the item. Where this results in items that are obviously too cheap or expensive, adjustments are made. Volunteers and dietary employees are allowed to eat for a reduced price and total approximately 55 individuals for lunch and dinner and 15 individuals for breakfast. Cashiers count out their banks,($50 in small bills and change) prior to service and then sit with a manager after the meal service has ended to reconcile sales (+ the bank) with the cash register tape. No action is taken against cashiers as long as their cash drawer is within $1.00 of the amount indicated on the cash register tape.

Customer surveys in the cafeteria indicate that the clientele really love the fresh bakery products and the free refills on sodas. There are also a dozen or so signature items served by cafeteria workers that are favorites of the cafeteria clientele. Most of these items are ethnic specialties created by the production workers. In many cases, no official recipes exist for these items but workers seem to know how to make them and they are very well received. Workers have coined catchy names for these items and take great pride in their creations. The most frequent complaints center around the long wait to get food and the difficulty finding seats during peak times. In addition to cafeteria service, vending machines, managed by Vending International Corporation, are located in a cove off the lobby and offer a limited selection of snack foods and sandwiches. Many employees appear to go to neighboring food service establishments for lunch or dinner.

Food Purchasing/Receiving/Storage

Food is purchased by Jack for all areas of the operation. Jack uses a par stock system to purchase most foods and orders meat and specialty items based on menu requirements. He uses two different vendors for meats and checks prices weekly, ordering from the vendor that offers the lowest price overall. Meats are delivered a minimum of twice weekly. Plantation Sysco is the vendor used for most staple items; orders are sent to the vendor through a computer link three times a week. Produce is purchased from Harvest House twice weekly. Dairy products, eggs, and bread are standing orders, with products delivered on a daily basis. Purchasing specifications exist for most perishable items, but they seem to simply be collecting dust. Due to the very limited amount of storage space, vendors are often delivering food in the morning for use at that day's evening meal or the next day's lunch.

When products arrive, Kelly (the storeroom clerk) checks them in, dates and signs for the items, and distributes them to the appropriate storage area. If Kelly is not available, the kitchen supervisor signs the invoice. Most items are delivered in the morning hours and some days are much more hectic than others. Kelly checks items in by counting at least one box of the item in question and visually inspecting a sample of products for quality. She also checks temperatures of cold items when possible. Standing orders are handled completely by the vendor. The bread vendor brings the same types of bread and amounts every day as directed by Jack when the order was set up. This order is reviewed and adjusted yearly or when menu changes are made. The dairy vendor has been given a par level for the milk and eggs. When stocks fall below the par level, they are replenished. The dairy vendor is responsible for checking stocks in the operation, leaving the appropriate amount of each item and delivering the invoice to Kelly, who signs it.

The storage areas consist of a dry goods storeroom, two walk-in refrigerators, and several smaller reach-in refrigerators in the production and service areas. Meat, chicken, and fish are stored on the top shelves of the production area walk-in refrigerator so that these products will be accessible to the production team. Leftovers are also stored in this refrigerator, since reheating equipment is nearby. Expensive items such as lobster and filet mignon are kept in a locked cage inside the production walk-in refrigerator. Kelly and Jack are the only individuals with keys to the cage. A physical inventory system is used with inventories taken weekly. To complete the inventory, Kelly and Jack work together to count and record the number of items in stock. Cost of food used is calculated bi-weekly by adding beginning inventory to purchases and then subtracting ending inventory.

As previously mentioned, all items received are dated; prepared foods are also dated if not served immediately. If prepared foods are for modified diets, this is also indicated on the label. Milk is stored in the dairy walk-in until time of service. Immediately prior to the trayline, milk is placed on sheet pans in a mobile rack and wheeled out to the trayline area for tray assembly. The production area walk-in is maintained at 40 degrees Fahrenheit and the dairy walk-in is kept at 45 degrees Fahrenheit. Temperatures are checked each morning by the morning supervisor and recorded accordingly. If temperatures are not meeting standards, a maintenance request is submitted.

Enteral feeding products are purchased by the dietary department and distributed to patients as ordered. Patients are billed through pharmacy for enteral products ordered by physicians. A formulary has been developed that lists all available enteral formulas carried by the department. If a physician orders a product that is not on the formulary, he or she is notified that the product is not available and a substitute product is recommended.

Food Production

The majority of the food for the cafeteria and regular patient diets is prepared from scratch. Standardized recipes are religiously used for modified diets but often ignored for regular patient diets and cafeteria. Panning charts are in place and followed for all meals. Forecasting of items needed for patient services is done by the evening diet clerk based on her experience and input from the cooks. There tend to be considerable leftovers on most days but once or twice a week the trayline will run short on an item and a substitution will have to be made. Cafeteria forecasting is done by the cafeteria supervisor based on previous sales records. Leftover items from the patient trayline are often served in the cafeteria at the next meal but the majority of leftovers are discarded.

Utility and Warewashing

A crew of utility workers runs the dishmachine and pot wash areas. Trayline workers help on the dishmachine after all trays have been served and they have taken their break. A chemical sanitizer is used in the dishmachine during the final rinse cycle whenever it is available. When it is not available, dishes

7

are run through the machine twice to assure that they are adequately cleaned. Temperatures for the dishmachine are 120 degrees Fahrenheit for the wash cycle and 140 degrees Fahrenheit for the rinse and final rinse cycles. All dishes and trays from patient services and the cafeteria are run through the dishmachine, thus the cafeteria can often run low on trays during service if the dishmachine crew is not operating at full capacity. Pots are washed in a three-section sink and chemical sanitizer is used in the third sink.

Recruitment/Hiring/Training/Evaluation

In general, when positions open at the hospital, the personnel department recruits and screens applicants. The department with the opening then interviews applicants who were not screened out and recommends someone for hiring. If the Personnel Department agrees, this individual is offered the position. If he or she accepts, then he or she undergoes an employee physical and begins working. All employees are expected to attend hospital orientation, but it is only offered four times per year. Thus, employees often have been working at the hospital for several weeks before they attend this all-day session. Once an individual is hired, a three-month probationary period ensues where the employment can be discontinued without all the usual documentation and review. After three months, the individual is given an evaluation. If it is acceptable, the probation period ends and the employee has all the rights and responsibilities of a regular employee. In accordance with personnel policies, employees are evaluated once yearly at the anniversary of their hiring date.

In the food and nutrition services department, most individuals who are hired heard of the position from a friend in the department. This is partially due to the fact that managers encourage workers to let their friends know about positions that open up in the department. During the interview, individuals are asked to read the menu to assure that they can read English. They are also asked about previous related experience and reasons for seeking out this type of employment. (Most individuals seek out hospital foodservice employment over other foodservice employment due to regular hours and availability of benefits.) Applicants are informed of the number of hours expected and the need for flexibility in scheduling. References are checked prior to hiring someone but often references are simply personal friends of the applicant. When individuals are hired, they are given a brief half-hour orientation to the job and then are assigned to a seasoned employee for on-the-job training. To optimize the possibility for success, the new employee is only asked to master a few skills in the first few days and is not actually expected to work a full position for several weeks. Two to three additional key employees are also identified and asked to assist the new worker by checking frequently with him or her and taking him or her under their wings. Almost all employees survive the probationary period and the evaluation at the end of the three-month period is usually treated as a formality. Turnover in the department is consistent with other similar operations.

Clinical Services

Three dietitians are presently on staff at Inlet Isles, who spend the vast majority of their day doing nutritional assessments, advising regarding enteral and parenteral nutrition, and providing counseling to patients at discharge. At present, there is very little outpatient counseling, but dietitians will provide this service for a fee of $40 per hour. Naturally, this money is counted as general revenue for the department. Dietitians see patients if a doctor orders a consult or if the patient is identified through the normal screening procedure. The screening procedure mandates that a person be seen within 24 hours if he or she is on a calculated diet, within three days if on any other modified diet or texturally altered diet, and within seven days for all patients. Standards are in place regarding the care of patients for most major diet modifications and disease states. The chief dietitian pulls medical records every six months to check for compliance to the above policies and standards. Dietitians stay very busy during the day but manage to visit and care for patients in accordance to the visitation policy at least 90 percent of the time. Presently, the administration is considering a lay-off and a clinical dietitian position is expected to be one of the first positions to be cut.

FOODSERVICE MENUS

The patient menu is a seven-day select cycle menu. The items with stars by them are the items given to patients who cannot or do not choose to select their meals. The cafeteria uses this basic menu as well but provides a daily special to reduce monotony.

Condiments for the breakfast meal include:

Margarine*
Butter
Syrup
Jelly*
Lemon
Non-Dairy Creamer*
Sugar*
Sugar Substitute
Salt*
Pepper*
Cream Cheese

Condiments for the lunch and dinner meal include:

Margarine*
Butter
Jelly
Lemon
Non-Dairy Creamer
Sugar
Sugar Substitute
Salt*
Pepper*
Salad Dressing
Catsup

Recipe items can be found in *Food for Fifty* (see reference list for full citation).

Day One

Breakfast	Lunch	Dinner
Fruits and Juices 　Orange Juice* 　Apple Juice 　Prune Juice 　Stewed Prunes 　Pineapple Chunks **Cereals** 　Puffed Rice 　Corn Pops 　Oatmeal* 　Cream of Wheat **Entrees** 　Poached Egg* 　Creamed Dried Beef 　Blueberry Pancakes **Breads** 　White Toast* 　Wheat Toast 　Cornmeal Muffin 　Plain Muffin 　Multigrain Bagel **Beverages** 　Whole Milk 　Lowfat Milk* 　Skim Milk 　Coffee* 　Decaf Coffee 　Tea 　Hot Chocolate	**Soups** 　Beef Broth 　Broccoli-Cheese* 　Beef Noodle **Salads** 　Waldorf* 　Spinach and Mushroom **Cold Sandwich** 　Chicken Salad **Entrees** 　Tuna and Noodles* 　Broccoli and Cheese Casserole **Side Dishes** 　Baked Potato 　Rice Pilaf* 　Ranch Style Beans* 　Peas and Carrots **Breads** 　White 　Wheat 　Saltine Crackers* **Desserts** 　Banana 　Chocolate Pudding* 　Date Bars **Beverages** 　Whole Milk 　Lowfat Milk 　Skim Milk 　Coffee 　Decaf Coffee 　Hot Tea 　Iced Tea 　Soda* 　Diet Soda 　Fruit Juice	**Soups** 　Chicken Broth 　Cream of Asparagus 　Pepper Pot* **Salads** 　Apple-Carrot 　Sliced Tomatoes* **Entrees** 　Baked Ham 　Salmon Loaf* 　Pasta with Vegetable Sauce **Side Dishes** 　New Potatoes* 　Mexican Rice 　Glazed Carrots* 　Seasoned Cauliflower **Breads** 　White 　Wheat 　Dinner Roll* **Desserts** 　Melon Balls 　Vanilla Frozen Yogurt 　Pineapple Upside-Down Cake* **Beverages** 　Whole Milk 　Lowfat Milk 　Skim Milk 　Coffee 　Decaf Coffee 　Hot Tea 　Iced Tea* 　Soda 　Diet Soda 　Fruit Juice

Day Two

Breakfast	Lunch	Dinner
Fruits and Juices Orange Juice* Grape Juice Tomato Juice Pear Halves Sliced Melon **Cereals** Shredded Wheat Total Oatmeal* Grits **Entrees** Hard Cooked Egg* Scrapple Doughnuts **Breads** White Toast* Wheat Toast Raisin Nut Muffin Plain Muffin Banana Walnut Bagel **Beverages** Whole Milk Lowfat Milk* Skim Milk Coffee* Decaf Coffee Tea Hot Chocolate	**Soups** Chicken Broth Cream of Cauliflower Tomato Rice* **Salads** Pear with Cottage Cheese* Cucumber-Tomato **Cold Sandwich** Ham and Cheese* **Entrees** Ham Patties Spinach Quiche **Side Dishes** Oven-Browned Potatoes* Broccoli Rice Au Gratin Green Beans* Succotash **Breads** White Wheat Saltine Crackers* **Desserts** Sliced Peaches Vanilla Frozen Yogurt Oatmeal Raisin Cookies* **Beverages** Whole Milk Lowfat Milk Skim Milk Coffee Decaf Coffee Hot Tea Iced Tea Soda* Diet Soda Fruit Juice	**Soups** Beef Broth Cheese Soup Turkey Vegetable* **Salads** Grapefruit-Orange Tossed Greens* **Entrees** Salisbury Steak* Chicken and Snow Peas Spinach Lasagna **Side Dishes** Baked Stuffed Potato* White Rice Peas with Pearl Onions* Broiled Tomatoes **Breads** White Wheat Dinner Roll* **Desserts** Queen Anne Cherries Butterscotch Pudding Chocolate Cake* **Beverages** Whole Milk Lowfat Milk Skim Milk Coffee Decaf Coffee Hot Tea Iced Tea* Soda Diet Soda Fruit Juice

Day Three

Breakfast	Lunch	Dinner
Fruits and Juices Orange Juice* Apple Juice Cranberry Juice Applesauce Fruit Cocktail **Cereals** Raisin Bran Granola Oatmeal Cream of Wheat* **Entrees** Cheese Omelet* Sausage Waffles **Breads** White Toast* Wheat Toast Blueberry Muffin Plain Muffin Cinnamon Raisin Bagel **Beverages** Whole Milk Lowfat Milk* Skim Milk Coffee* Decaf Coffee Tea Hot Chocolate	**Soups** Beef Broth Cream of Tomato* Split Pea **Salads** Fruit Cocktail* Coleslaw **Cold Sandwich** Turkey and Swiss Cheese **Entrees** Chicken a la King* Mushroom Quiche **Side Dishes** White Rice* Fried Potatoes Zucchini and Summer Squash Buttered Corn* **Breads** White Wheat Saltine Crackers* **Desserts** Apple Chocolate Ice Cream* Chocolate Chip Cookies **Beverages** Whole Milk Lowfat Milk Skim Milk Coffee Decaf Coffee Hot Tea Iced Tea Soda* Diet Soda Fruit Juice	**Soups** Chicken Broth Cream of Spinach Chicken Noodle* **Salads** Gelatin with Fruit* Green Pepper Slaw **Entrees** Spaghetti and Meat Balls Fillet of Sole* Sicilian Rice and Vegetables **Side Dishes** Potato Rosettes* Scalloped Corn Broccoli with Cheese Sauce* Harvard Beets **Breads** White Wheat Dinner Roll* **Desserts** Banana Strawberry Ice Cream Cherry Pie* **Beverages** Whole Milk Lowfat Milk Skim Milk Coffee Decaf Coffee Hot Tea Iced Tea* Soda Diet Soda Fruit Juice

Day Four

Breakfast	Lunch	Dinner
Fruits and Juices Orange Juice* Grape Juice Pineapple Juice Fried Banana Sliced Peaches	**Soups** Chicken Broth Cream of Celery* Navy Bean	**Soups** Beef Broth Cream of Mushroom Beef Barley*
Cereals Wheaties Corn Flakes* Oatmeal Grits	**Salads** Sliced Peaches Carrot and Celery Sticks*	**Salads** Peach and Cottage Cheese* Tossed Greens
Entrees Fried Egg* Ham French Toast	**Cold Sandwich** Egg Salad **Entrees** Beef Stroganoff* Vegetable Chow Mein	**Entrees** Beef Stew Herb-Marinated Chicken* Baked Ziti
Breads White Toast* Wheat Toast Banana Muffin Plain Muffin Blueberry Bagel	**Side Dishes** Buttered Noodles* Steamed Rice Baked Acorn Squash Spinach*	**Side Dishes** Oven-Browned Potatoes* Baked Sweet Potato Seasoned Brussels Sprouts* Turnips with Peas
Beverages Whole Milk Lowfat Milk* Skim Milk Coffee* Decaf Coffee Tea Hot Chocolate	**Breads** White Wheat Saltine Crackers*	**Breads** White Wheat Dinner Roll*
	Desserts Pear Halves Banana Pudding* Angel Food Cake	**Desserts** Plums Tapioca Pudding* Pound Cake/Strawberry Sauce
	Beverages Whole Milk Lowfat Milk Skim Milk Coffee Decaf Coffee Hot Tea Iced Tea Soda* Diet Soda Fruit Juice	**Beverages** Whole Milk Lowfat Milk Skim Milk Coffee Decaf Coffee Hot Tea Iced Tea* Soda Diet Soda Fruit Juice

15

Day Five

Breakfast	Lunch	Dinner
Fruits and Juices Orange Juice* Grape Juice Cranapple Juice Cantaloupe Grapefruit Half **Cereals** Cheerios* Wheaties Oatmeal Grits **Entrees** Mushroom Omelet* Sausage and Egg Bake Glazed Doughnut **Breads** White Toast* Wheat Toast Apple Nut Muffin Plain Muffin Whole Wheat Bagel **Beverages** Whole Milk Lowfat Milk* Skim Milk Coffee* Decaf Coffee Tea Hot Chocolate	**Soups** Chicken Broth Cream of Pea Chicken Rice* **Salads** Pineapple Cheese* Creamy Coleslaw **Cold Sandwich** Club Sandwich **Entrees** Chicken and Noodles* Spanish Omelet **Side Dishes** Steamed Rice Oven Browned Potatoes* Baked Tomatoes Peas with Mushrooms* **Breads** White Wheat Saltine Crackers* **Desserts** Apple Orange Sherbet Peanut Butter Cookies* **Beverages** Whole Milk Lowfat Milk Skim Milk Coffee Decaf Coffee Hot Tea Iced Tea Soda* Diet Soda Fruit Juice	**Soups** Beef Broth Cream of Vegetable Tomato Barley* **Salads** Grapefruit Apple Tossed Vegetable* **Entrees** Turkey Tetrazzini* Seafood Quiche Vegetarian Spaghetti **Side Dishes** Buttered Noodles* Lemon-Seasoned Potatoes Savory Carrots* Creole Green Beans **Breads** White Wheat Dinner Roll* **Desserts** Orange Sections Chocolate Chip Ice Cream Apple Crumb Pie* **Beverages** Whole Milk Lowfat Milk Skim Milk Coffee Decaf Coffee Hot Tea Iced Tea* Soda Diet Soda Fruit Juice

Day Six

Breakfast	Lunch	Dinner

Breakfast

Fruits and Juices
Orange Juice*
Apple Juice
Cran-Grape Juice
Apricot Halves
Sliced Peaches

Cereals
Corn Flakes*
Rice Krispies
Oatmeal
Cream of Wheat

Entrees
Scrambled Eggs with Cheese*
Sausage Biscuit
Coffee Cake

Breads
White Toast*
Wheat Toast
Oatmeal Muffin
Plain Muffin
Egg Bagel

Beverages
Whole Milk
Lowfat Milk*
Skim Milk
Coffee*
Decaf Coffee
Tea
Hot Chocolate

Lunch

Soups
Chicken Broth
Cream of Broccoli
Beef Barley*

Salads
Peach with Cottage
Cheese*
Triple Bean

Cold Sandwich
Tuna Salad

Entrees
Beef Pot Pie*
Broccoli Rice au Gratin

Side Dishes
Mashed Potatoes*
Scalloped Corn
Green Beans*
Peas and Cauliflower

Breads
White
Wheat
Saltine Crackers*

Desserts
Pear
Coconut Pudding
Applesauce Cake*

Beverages
Whole Milk
Lowfat Milk
Skim Milk
Coffee
Decaf Coffee
Hot Tea
Iced Tea
Soda*
Diet Soda
Fruit Juice

Dinner

Soups
Beef Broth
Cream of Mushroom Barley*
Chicken Gumbo

Salads
Sunshine Salad*
Marinated Carrots

Entrees
Baked Pork Chops*
Lemon Baked Fish Fillets
Pasta Primavera

Side Dishes
Rice Pilaf
Duchess Potatoes*
Butternut Squash with Apples
Seasoned Zucchini*

Breads
White
Wheat
Dinner Roll*

Desserts
Mixed Fruit Cocktail
Chocolate Frozen Yogurt*
Gingersnaps

Beverages
Whole Milk
Lowfat Milk
Skim Milk
Coffee
Decaf Coffee
Hot Tea
Iced Tea*
Soda
Diet Soda
Fruit Juice

Day Seven

Breakfast	Lunch	Dinner

Breakfast

Fruits and Juices
Orange Juice*
Apple Juice
Grapefruit Juice
Orange Slices
Grapefruit Half

Cereals
Cheerios
Rice Krispies
Oatmeal*
Cream of Wheat

Entrees
Scrambled Egg*
Bacon
Pancakes

Breads
White Toast*
Wheat Toast
Apple Muffin
Plain Muffin
Plain Bagel

Beverages
Whole Milk
Lowfat Milk*
Skim Milk
Coffee*
Decaf Coffee
Tea
Hot Chocolate

Lunch

Soups
Beef Broth
Cream of Potato*
Vegetable Beef

Salads
Gelatin with Fruit*
Tossed Green Salad

Cold Sandwich
Bacon, Lettuce and Tomato

Entrees
Scalloped Turkey*
Macaroni and Cheese

Side Dishes
Buttered Rice*
Baked Cheese Grits
Seasoned Carrots*
Lima Beans

Breads
White
Wheat
Saltine Crackers*

Desserts
Grapes
Strawberry Ice Cream
Chocolate Brownie*

Beverages
Whole Milk
Lowfat Milk
Skim Milk
Coffee
Decaf Coffee
Hot Tea
Iced Tea
Soda*
Diet Soda
Fruit Juice

Dinner

Soups
Chicken Broth
Cream of Chicken*
Minestrone

Salads
Apple-Cabbage*
Carrot-Raisin

Entrees
Meat Loaf*
Chicken Cacciatore
Swiss Broccoli Pasta

Side Dishes
Mashed Potatoes*
Buttered Noodles
Steamed Asparagus*
Baked Eggplant

Breads
White
Wheat
Dinner Roll*

Desserts
Orange Sections
Chocolate Ice Cream
Apple Crisp*

Beverages
Whole Milk
Lowfat Milk
Skim Milk
Coffee
Decaf Coffee
Hot Tea
Iced Tea*
Soda
Diet Soda
Fruit Juice

FINANCIAL INFORMATION

This section includes a budget for the fiscal year and a sample weekly operating report for week 10 of the fiscal year. The weekly operating report can also be found on the enclosed disk. The weekly operating report contains the information commonly found on an income statement, with specific statistics common to hospital foodservices.

Department of Food and Nutrition Services Yearly Budget

Revenues

Cash	
Cafeteria Sales	530,000
Outpatient Counseling	10,000
Paper Transfer	
Floor Stocks	62,600
Nourishments/TF	46,000
Total Revenue	648,600

Expenses

Food	730,808
Labor	1,495,624
Tubefeedings	23,348
Cleaning Supplies	11,860
Silverware and China	6,000
Paper Supplies	40,480
Kitchen Utensils and	
Non-Capital Equipment	3,720
Maintenance Contracts	470 (cash registers)
Equipment Rental	3,000 (yogurt machine)
Uniforms	1,660
Office Supplies	5,550
Photocopying	410
Postage	125
Print Shop	3,100
Instructional Materials	220
Books and Periodicals	500
Travel and Registrations	2,100
Total Expenses	2,328,975

Weekly Operating Report Description

The next two pages represent the weekly operating report (WOR) for week 10 of the fiscal year. This report is commonly used in foodservice and contains information traditionally found on an income statement. This report is also contained on the enclosed disk as an Excel spreadsheet (file name: WOR(week 10 operating report)). The template used for this weekly operating report can be found in Lynne Richard's book entitled *Measure It, Manage It,* which is published by the American Dietetic Association (1997). Please refer to this reference for further clarification about the content and design of this report.

Terminology

YTD	=	year to date
MEC	=	meal equivalent cost (the cost of an average meal)
MEP	=	meal equivalent price (the price of an average meal)
RFCost	=	raw food cost
FTE	≈	full time equivalent
PPM	=	per patient meal
PPD	=	per patient day

Section A

This section outlines the cost of the food purchased and used during the week. Prior year to date and year to date information is also provided.

Section B

The meals columns of section B (columns B and C) refer to number of meals, served or "equivalent" meals, served in each area. Column D gives the raw food cost for those meals, whereas column E gives the budgeted costs. Columns F and G provide actual and budgeted sales data for all areas that are either billed out at cost or billed out/sold for a profit.

Section C

This section gives basic statistics on labor, customers, and sales data.

Section D

This section represents the typical income statement. Much of the data is drawn from the previous section. Various costs and revenues are listed with actual as well as budgeted dollars listed. Per patient meal (PPM) and per patient day (PPD) calculations are made when appropriate. The PPD net expense information represents the traditional "cost per patient day" amount per week and YTD.

Weekly Operating Report

OPERATING	REPORT	WEEK	TEN					
Section A								
Food Cost	meat	dairy	bakery	beverage	grocery	frsh/froz		Total
purchase	4,695	1,650	1,292	904	4,808	1,376		14,725
+ beg inv	1,396	304	145	388	2,240	136		4,609
subtotal	6,091	1,954	1,437	1,292	7,048	1,512		19,334
– end inv	1,662	252	131	267	1,823	162		4,297
total cost	4,429	1,702	1,306	1,025	5,225	1,350		15,037
priorYTD	37,720	14,820	11,335	9,170	46,975	11,750		131,770
YTD total	42,149	16,522	12,641	10,195	52,200	13,100		146,807
YTD budgeted	41,500	12,950	12,550	10,290	49,950	13,305		140,545
cost/meal	0	0	0	0	0	0		1.37
cost/meal to date								1.34
Section B	MEC >	1.35	MEP >	2.70				
Meals, Costs and Charges	meals	meals	RFCost	RFCost	Sale/chgs	Sale/chgs		
	Actual	Budget	Actual	Budget	Actual	Budget		
Patient	5,782	5,896						
Outpatient	0	0						
Pt Guest	45	50						
Floor Stck	896	892	1,210	1,204	1,210	1,204		
Nourishments	156	207	210	280	210	280		
Tubefeedings	453	449	612	606	612	606		
Subtotal (pt)	7,332	7,494	2,032	2,090	2,032	2,090		
cafe sales/chg	3,658	3,775	4,938	5,096	9,877	10,192		
vending sales	0	0	0	0	0	0		
catering sales	0	0	0	0	0	0		
other sales	0	0	0	0	0	0		
oupt. counsel					210	192		
subtotal (csh)	3,658	3,775	4,938	5,096	10,087	10,384		
catering charges	0	0	0	0	0	0		
other charges	0	0	0	0	0	0		
other charges	0	0	0	0	0	0		
subtotal (charge)	0	0	0	0	0	0		
Total	10,990	11,269	6,970	7,186	12,119	12,474		
prior YTD total	98,860	101,421	62,740	64,674	109,210	112,266		
YTD total	109,850	112,690	69,710	71,860	121,329	124,740		
Section C								
Statistics	Actual	Budget	per meal	per pt. day				
labor hours (reg)	2,351	2,340	0.214	1.280				
overtime	19	0	0.002	0.010				
subtotal (Prod hrs)	2,370	2,340	0.216	1.290				
vac., hol., sick	32	0	0.003	0.017				
total paid hours	2,402	2,340	0.219	1.308				
total FTE	60	59						
prior YTD prod hrs	21,840	21,060						
YTD prod hours	24,210	23,400	0.220	1.313				
prior YTD paid hrs	21,850	21,060						
YTD paid hours	24,252	23,400	0.221	1.316				

OPERATING	REPORT	WEEK	TEN					
Cust count	8,015							
prior YTD count	72,090							
YTD Count	80,105							
Cafe $/count	1.23							
Cafe $/day	1,411							
$ nourishPPM	0.04							
$ nourishPPD	0.11							
rev/wrk hr	5.11							
floor stk PP	0.66							
Section D								
Expense Summary								
	Actual	PM	PPD	Budget	PM	PPD		
Patient days	1,837			1,968				
prior YTD pt. days	16,595			17,718				
YTD pt days	18,432			19,686				
Cash sales	10,087		5.49	10,384		5.28		
prior YTD cash	93,994			93,456				
YTD cash	104,081			103,840				
charge revenue	2,032		1.11	2,090		1.06		
prior YTD charges	18,664			18,810				
YTD charges	20,696		1.12	20,900		1.06		
total food cost	15,037		8.19	14,054		7.14		
prior YTD food cost	131,770			126,491				
YTD food cost	146,807			140,545				
Total Labor	29,456		16.03	28,762		14.61		
prior YTD labor	264,155		15.92	258,858				
YTD labor	293,611		15.93	287,620				
uniforms	32			32				
cleaning	210			228				
paper	744			779				
tubefeedings	453			449				
utensils/replace	54			72				
rental	57			57				
travel/registration	0			40				
repairs, maint	0			9				
office / postage	124			109				
books/periodicals	24			10				
print/copies/instruct	76			72				
silver/china	106			115				
total expense	46,373		25.24	44,788		22.76		
less total revenue	12,119		6.60	12,474		6.34		
net expense	34,254	3.12	18.65	32,314	2.87	16.42		
prior YTD total exp	414,962			400,698				
prior YTD revenues	108,986			112,266				
YTD total expense	461,335		25.03	445,486		22.63		
less YTD revenues	121,105		6.57	124,740		6.34		
YTD net expenses	340,230	3.10	18.46	320,746	2.85	16.29		

23

STAFFING INFORMATION

This section contains:

- The list of positions that need to be filled in order to run the operation at full staffing.
- A chart of employees and the areas in which they are trained to work.
- A master schedule form for devising a two-week schedule for the operation. The schedule is also on disk as an Excel file with the file name: schedule form

Daily Operational Positions

Trayline   (441 hours per week)

T1 = trayline worker 1	6:45 AM–3:15 PM
T2 = trayline worker 2	6:45 AM–3:15 PM
T3 = trayline worker 3	6:45 AM–3:15 PM
T4 = trayline worker 4	6:45 AM–3:15 PM
T5 = trayline worker 5	6:45 AM–3:15 PM

T6 = trayline worker 6	3:00 PM–8:00 PM
T7 = trayline worker 7	3:00 PM–8:00 PM
T8 = trayline worker 8	3:00 PM–8:00 PM
T9 = trayline worker 9	4:00 PM–8:00 PM
T10 = trayline worker 10	4:00 PM–8:00 PM

Patient Service Supervisors   (112 hours per week)

| TS1 = morning supervisor | 6:30 AM–3:00 PM |
| TS2 = evening supervisor | 11:30 AM–8:00 PM |

Hosts/Hostesses (tray delivery and pickup)   (210 hours per week)

H1 = hostess 1	7:30 AM–6:30 PM
H2 = hostess 2	7:30 AM–6:30 PM
H3 = hostess 3	8:00 AM–7:00 PM

Diet Office   (208 hours per week)

DS = diet office supervisor	9:00 AM–5:30 PM (weekdays only)
D1 = diet office clerk 1	6:30 AM–3:00 PM
D2 = diet office clerk 2	11:00 AM–7:30 PM
D3 = diet office clerk 3	7:00 AM–3:30 PM

Cafeteria   (264 hours per week)

S1 = Server 1	6:00 AM–2:30 PM
S2 = Server 2	10:30 AM–7:00 PM
C1 = Cashier 1	6:00 AM–2:30 PM

| C2 = Cashier 2 | 11:30 AM–8:00 PM |
| CS = Supervisor | 10:00 AM–6:30 PM (weekdays only) |

Production   (544 hours per week)

PS = supervisor	8:30 AM–5:00 PM (weekdays only)
C1 = cook 1	9:00 AM–5:30 PM
C2 = cook 2	6:00 AM–2:30 PM
C3 = cook 3	6:00 AM–2:30 PM
C4 = cook 4	12:00 PM–8:30 PM
C5 = cook 5	10:00 AM–6:30 PM
B1 = baker	6:30 AM–3:00 PM
S1 = salads 1	8:00 AM–4:30 PM
S2 = salads 2	8:00 AM–4:30 PM
S3 = salads 3	11:00 AM–7:30 PM

Storeroom and Purchasing   (40 hours per week)

SR = storeroom / purchasing clerk 1   7:00 AM–3:30 PM (weekdays only)

Utility   (244 hours per week)

(bring up trays, dishmachine, pot wash, equipment, and general cleaning)

U1 = utility position 1	8:30 AM–5:00 PM
U2 = utility position 2	8:30 AM–5:00 PM
U3 = utility position 3	10:00 AM–6:30 PM
U4 = utility position 4	1:00 PM–9:00 PM
U5 = utility position 5	5:00 PM–9:00 PM (weekdays only)

Secretary   (40 hours per week)

Sec = secretary 1   8:30 AM–5:00 PM (weekdays only)

Management Team   (240 hours per week)

CD1 = clinical dietitian position one
CD2 = clinical dietitian position two
CD3 = clinical dietitian position three
AD1 = assistant director position one (patient services)
AD2 = assistant director position two (nonpatient services)
FSD = foodservice director

Employees and Their Training

Status	Job Class	Name	Trayline	Hostess	Caf. server	Utility
FT	FSW1	Cynthia	x			
FT	FSW1	Velma	x			
FT	FSW1	Dorothy	x			
FT	FSW1	Julia	x			
FT	FSW1	Leslie	x	x		
FT	FSW1	Iris	x			
FT	FSW1	Ginny	x	x		
FT	FSW1	Sheryl	x		x	
FT	FSW1	Karen	x	x		
FT	FSW1	Debra		x		
FT	FSW1	Eliza		x		
PT	FSW1	Chris	x			
PT	FSW1	George	x			
PT	FSW1	Ingrid	x			
PT	FSW1	Suzanne	x	x		
PT	FSW1	Jennifer	x			
PT	FSW1	Carolyn	x			
PT	FSW1	John	x			x
PT	FSW1	Cathy	x	x		
PT	FSW1	Ricardo	x		x	x
PT	FSW1	Myra			x	
FT	FSW1	Louisa			x	
FT	FSW1	Josh			x	
FT	FSW1	Al				x
FT	FSW1	Benton				x
FT	FSW1	Jacque				x
FT	FSW1	George				x
FT	FSW1	Roger				x
PT	FSW1	Maude				x
PT	FSW1	Philippe				x

Employees and Their Training

Status	Job Class	Name	Cashier	Diet Office	Secretary	(Hostess)	(Trayline)
FT	FSW2	Elaine		x			
FT	FSW2	Maria		x			
FT	FSW2	Victoria		x			
FT	FSW2	Sally		x			
PT	FSW2	Jari	x	x		x	x
FT	FSW2	Tom		x		x	
FT	FSW2	Donna	x				
PT	FSW2	Gayle	x				
FT	FSW2	Allison	x				
FT	Sec	Julia			x		

Status	Job Class	Name	Cook	Baker	Salad	Storeroom	
FT	FSW3	Sam	x				
FT	FSW3	Bob	x				
FT	FSW3	Darryl	x				
FT	FSW3	Larry	x				
FT	FSW3	Jacob	x	x			
FT	FSW3	Tony	x				
FT	FSW3	Don		x			
FT	FSW3	Barry	x				
FT	FSW3	Kelly				x	
FT	FSW3	Lavinia			x		
FT	FSW3	Claudia			x		
FT	FSW3	Lynn			x		
PT	FSW3	Joyce			x		
FT	FSW3	Bill	x		x		

Status	Job Class	Name	Pt. service	Diet office	Cafeteria	Production	
FT	FSS	Barbara	X				
FT	FSS	Mark	X				
FT	FSS	Lucy	X				
FT	FSS	Suani		X			
FT	FSS	Steve				X	
FT	FSS	Manuel			X		

*pt. service supervisors are in charge of supervising all aspects of the operation on the weekends.

Status	Job Class	Name					
FT	Mgr	Alicia					
FT	Asst Mgr	Nancy					
FT	Asst Mgr	Jack					
FT	Dietitian	Margo					
FT	Dietitian	Shirley					
FT	Dietitian	Patrick					

Master Schedule Form

NAME	Sun	Mon	Tues	Wed	Thur	Fri	Sat	Sun	Mon	Tue	Wed	Thur	Fri	Sat

PROBLEMS AND ACTIVITIES

1.   Assume that you are a consultant and have been asked to provide a comprehensive evaluation of this operation. Read through the case study carefully, studying the organizational chart and staffing information. Make a list of all the strengths and weaknesses you can identify in this case.

2.   Make a schedule for the department for a two-week period, following the guidelines listed below.
     A. All positions must be filled every day—the census is fairly high now.

     B. Employees can only be scheduled for positions that they have been trained for. See the attached chart indicating which positions each person can work.

     C. Part-time employees can only work 32 hours per week maximum. It is best to work them 20 hours per week and no more if possible.

     D. Each full-time employee gets a minimum of one weekend out of three off from work. Employees should be scheduled on or off for the full weekend rather than splitting days.

     E. All full-time employees work 40 hours per week. Hostess positions require four 10-hour days with an additional hour for lunch/dinner. Other positions require five 8-hour days with an additional half hour for a meal.

     F. Try to avoid working employees more than five days in a row.

     G. Try to avoid having employees working late one day and early the next. This cannot always be avoided (i.e., relief supervisor position).

     After making the schedule, what changes would you make in the operation or employee base? Who do you think is your most valuable employee? Why? What could you do to make staffing the kitchen easier?

3.   The case study tells you that most of the food is prepared from scratch. What aspects of the budget confirm this fact? How would the budget differ if the food used was largely convenience food or food produced elsewhere and brought in already prepared?

4.   Alicia has noticed that her food cost is fairly high for a foodservice operation of this size and scope, so she calls in a management consultant to explore this problem and indicate if she is justified in her concerns. The management consultant assesses the situation and finds several possible causes for the high food costs and begins to investigate these trouble spots further.
     A. Look at the operating report for the end of week 10 for this facility. In what categories of food are you over budget year to date? What are the possible causes of your high food cost?

     B. Once possible causes have been identified, select five of these causes and indicate how you would investigate them to determine which factors actually were resulting in excessively high food costs.

     C. Select two root causes from the list of possible causes for the high food cost problem and develop alternatives for correcting the situation.

     D. What would your weekly operating report look like if your food costs were in line with the budgeted amount? Change the weekly operating report to assess this. How does correction of your food costs influence your cost per patient day?

31

5. Bill Higgins, the hospital administrator, approaches Alicia and informs her that the hospital is having serious financial troubles. He lets her know that costs need to be reduced and revenues need to be increased in her department and several others if the hospital is to continue to operate. Alicia points out to Bill that food costs have come down considerably after the department implemented many of the recommendations of the management consultant. Bill pats Alicia on the back and tells her that he appreciates her good work but that revenues need to increase as well if layoffs are to be avoided. After Alicia recovers from this blow, she pulls her management team together and asks them to draw up a marketing plan for increasing revenues.

    A. What marketing opportunities exist in this operation?

    B. Select a marketing opportunity and develop a marketing plan.

    C. Based on your plan, estimate the amount of money you could generate on a weekly and yearly basis. Adjust the budget to indicate the newly anticipated revenues and expenses. Pretend that you have implemented this and adjust the weekly operating report for week 10 to reflect these changes. What is the influence of the new revenue-generating opportunity on cost per patient day and cost per meal? Were you able to reduce the cost per patient day substantially with these changes? Were you able to reduce the cost per meal or per patient day substantially when you add this revenue generating activity to the cost reductions from better control of food (question 4)?

    D. Assume you have decided that the potential exists to increase outpatient counseling. Estimate the amount of money that can be generated from providing 20 additional hours of outpatient counseling per week at $40 per hour. Would this revenue cover the cost of a diet technician so that a dietitian can be freed up to move over to outpatient counseling on a half-time basis? How much money would be left over? What other expenses would be affected by this change?

6. Nancy Newbury has just conducted a patient survey and many of the patients stated that the hot food wasn't even warm and the cold food was room temperature! Nancy looks at the data from the dummy trays and finds that the temperatures are, indeed, unacceptable. She seeks out your advice.

    A. Based on what you know about this operation, what are the possible factors that could be responsible for food not being at the right temperature when it reaches the patient?

    B. How might you investigate to determine which of these possible causes is actually causing your temperature problem?

    C. Select three of these possible root causes and indicate what you might to do assure that the patients' hot foods are hot and cold foods are cold.

7. In preparation for the health department inspection, Alicia asks you to observe procedures for a day and report strengths and weaknesses with regard to the sanitation and safety procedures in this operation.

    A. What will your report identify as strengths and weaknesses?

    B. What recommendations will you make?

8. Nancy notes that almost 30 percent of patients order additional food after their tray has been delivered. This results in a large number of second trays, increased food costs, and exhaustion for the person preparing the additional trays. Nancy checks with other hospitals and finds that the number of late trays (trays sent after usual meal service) is closer to 5 to 10 percent and consists largely of individuals being newly admitted or coming off liquid diets. In Nancy's case, it seems that the patients just don't like what they originally got for lunch.

   A. Based on the information provided in this case study, why do you suspect that patients are rejecting the food being sent and requesting additional food?

   B. Why might patients not fill out their select menu? How might you investigate this situation to determine why patients aren't filling out their menus?

   C. Assume that you completed the survey and were able to identify one or two causes for the problem. Select one cause and indicate what could be done to increase the percentage of marked menus. Identify alternatives and discuss pros and cons of each alternative. Remember that each alternative must be possible within the context of this case.

   D. What final solution (or set of solutions) would you select to deal with this problem?

9. Thanks to your excellent problem solving, the percentage of marked menus has increased to 82 percent. Unfortunately, summary results from tray audits indicate a 72 percent accuracy rating when tray contents are compared against the menu. This suggests that more than 25 percent of patients at a given meal may not be getting exactly what they ordered. Patient survey results confirm a level of dissatisfaction with regard to tray accuracy with several patients stating "I rarely get what I ordered".

   A. Based on the information in this case study, what are some of the reasons that an individual might not get what he or she ordered?

   B. How might you investigate this to find out the true root cause of inaccuracies?

   C. Assuming that the problems identified in the first part of this question are indeed negatively impacting tray accuracy, what could be done to improve tray accuracy in the future?

10. Bill Higgins called Alicia today and told her that the director of nursing is complaining that nurses cannot get through the cafeteria line in time to eat and return to their units within one-half hour.

    A. If you were Bill Higgins, how might you address this problem?

    B. Based on the sequence of events here, how would you rate the relationship between the Food and Nutrition Services Department and the Nursing Department?

    C. What are some of the reasons why the relationship between these two departments is strained? What could be done to improve this relationship?

11. You are now in the role of Nancy Newbury. On Wednesday morning, Cynthia, Velma, Dorothy, Julia, and Iris all request to have this Saturday off to go to the funeral of a close friend of theirs. This reminds you of a time last year when four evening trayline workers wanted Friday evening off to go to their high school prom.

A. How will you respond to this request?

B. What would you do if the employees requesting Saturday off were Elaine, Maria, Victoria, and Sally? Could you cover for all these employees?

C. Why has this difficulty arisen (five people all wanting the same day off)? What should you do over the long run to reduce the number of times that a situation like this arises?

12. Roger always finishes washing pots sooner than the other utility employees so he takes a longer break. Although you are pleased that Roger is such an efficient worker, you know that other employees have observed that he gets a longer break and feel it is unfair. Eventually, Maude comes to you to complain.
A. What do you tell Maude?

B. What policy do you want to have in place regarding workers who finish their assigned duties quicker than expected and then take longer breaks?

13. In order to wash patient trays and dishes, an assembly line is set up with both trayline employees and utility employees participating. Some employees remove silverware while other employees dump trash, load the machine with dirty dishes, or unload the clean dishes at the other end of the machine. Put yourself in the role of Nancy Newbury. Lately you have noticed that Lucy occasionally stops the dishwashing process to tell a funny story or joke. You feel that this is improper but you are not sure what to do about this since Lucy runs the fastest and most accurate trayline and her crew also finishes washing dishes approximately 10 minutes earlier than crews led by the other two supervisors. Mostly, you are concerned about the appearance of things. What if an administrator came through the kitchen and saw Lucy telling a story while dirty dishes sat motionless on the conveyor belt. Is there a problem here? If a problem exists, what should be done about it?

14. A recent study indicated that the meals per labor hour for this operation is 1.3. This is fairly low and thus requires further analysis. There are legitimate reasons for a low meals per labor hour ratio, but there are also factors that could be adjusted to improve productivity.
A. Based on what you know about this operation, what factors contribute to the low meals per labor hour ratio?

B. Based on your list above, what factors that negatively influence productivity (meals per labor hour) do you feel are justifiable (in other words, they reduce productivity but the benefit makes it worthwhile so you wouldn't change these things)?

C. What aspects of the operation could be adjusted to improve productivity? How would each of the above adjustments influence the quality of care for the patient?

D. What are some other ways to measure productivity?

15. A hurricane is approaching. You have 36 hours to make preparations.
A. What information would you expect to find in the disaster plan?

B. What issues do you face with an impending disaster?

C. How might you adjust the menu if you had no power but still needed to feed patients and staff?

D. What items would you want to keep on hand in the storeroom for an occasion like this?

16. You are Jack Perry and you have been told by a confidential source that your cashiers are stealing from you.
A. What are the strengths and weaknesses in your present cash handling procedure?

B. How might you "catch" the cashiers stealing so you can verify this information?

C. How could you improve the cash handling process?

D. What else would you want to check on or monitor in order to be sure cash handling is optimal?

17. You are Jack Perry. Recently, a community nutritionist contacted you to let you know that there is a need for a meals on wheels program in your geographic region. She is requesting that you be the meal provider and she will coordinate volunteers for meal delivery. Your operation will need to provide the necessary equipment for meal delivery but volunteers will use their own cars to transport meals. She has approximately fifty eligible recipients lined up so she will need 100 meals total (fifty for lunch and fifty for dinner). The nutritionist feels that recipients will not be able to pay more than $25.00 per week for the service, which would include fourteen meals per week. No additional government funding is presently available. You have decided to participate since you realize that your operation is uniquely situated to meet this need. You do not need to add any labor for this service since it only requires an additional fifty trays and there is time to run these trays at the start of the lunch and dinner trayline.
A. In order to provide this service, what additional resources will you need?

B. How will the budget for your operation change once this program is implemented?

C. What aspects of the weekly operating report are likely to change?

D. Can you break even with this level of revenue? If not, can you cover your additional expenses?

E. What might be included in a cost-benefit analysis of this service?

18. This assignment is to be done using the seven-day cycle menu in the Inlet Isles case study. Take any two days in the cycle; be sure to specify which two days you are using. The items marked with an asterisk (*) indicate items that would be served to a patient who did not have a marked menu. (You may assume that these patients are on a normal diet.) Many of the menu items are from *Food for Fifty*. For those items, use the portion size given with the recipe. The portion sizes for other items are listed below.

Juices, 4 oz.

Food for Fifty 11/e by Molt, © 2001. Reprinted by permission of Prentice-Hall, Inc., Upper Saddle River, NJ.

Fruits and vegetables, ½ cup or 1 piece
Cereals, 1 cup
Breads and rolls, 1 piece
Beverages, 8 oz; sodas, 12 oz.
Margarine, 1 Tbsp.
Jelly, 1 Tbsp.
Creamer, 1 oz.
Sugar, 1 tsp.
Salt, ½ tsp.
Pepper, 1/4 tsp.
Crackers, 4 each
Salad Dressing, 1 Tbsp.
Lemon, 1/8 lemon
Sandwich, 2 slices bread, 1 oz. each meat and cheese
Puddings/ice cream, ½ cup

A. Using a computerized diet analysis program, compare the starred items to the RDA for an adult female, age 25–50. Analyze each day separately. Be sure to include starred condiments listed on the page introducing the menus. Make a table listing the RDA (or recommended amount) in one column, the amount of each nutrient in the second column, and the %RDA in the third column. Evaluate all nutrients for which there is an RDA, plus total carbohydrates, sugars, fat, saturated fat, and percent of calories from fat. Which nutrients are low? Which are high? How significant is this?

B. Using the same two days, evaluate and describe the aesthetic quality of the menu made up of the starred items (color, texture, flavor, etc.). Would you substitute any of the other items *on the menu* for any of the starred items? Why? Keep in mind the patient population.

C. Using the same two days, what changes, if any, would you recommend in the overall menu? Would you add any new foods or eliminate any foods altogether? Why?

D. What are some possible sources of error in your nutrient analysis?

E. Describe the advantages and disadvantages of using a seven-day cycle menu. Address the impact of using a seven-day cycle menu versus a six-day or eight-day cycle menu.

19. This assignment is to be done using the first five days of the seven-day cycle menu in the Inlet Isles case study. These days can be labeled Monday through Friday. Develop three menus of finger foods, one each appropriate for the dialysis unit, the daycare center, and the outpatient clinic.

Patients typically spend several hours undergoing dialysis. They don't eat during the procedure, but are offered a snack before they leave. For the daycare center, the children (ages 2–5) bring their lunches, but the hospital provides morning and afternoon snacks. The outpatient clinic has patients throughout the day, as well as family members/caregivers, and offers various food items for sale in the clinic, as an alternative to going to the cafeteria. Each of these centers has a household-size refrigerator, but no other foodservice/food preparation equipment.

Keep in mind the audiences and which foods are appropriate for them, what is being served to the hospitalized patients on those days, and the resources available in the hospital. The menus may overlap with the patient menus and with each other. Don't forget to include beverages as appropriate. Present each menu in an attractive format.

20. The Inlet Isles Hospital supports heart healthy and weight loss classes periodically conducted for staff. In addition, many of the hospital staff are under a physician's care for hypertension, diabetes, and so on. A group of staff representing most of the departments presented a complaint to Alicia Deerborne, Foodservice Director. They report that there are very few low-calorie, low-fat, high-fiber foods offered on the menu in the cafeteria, especially at lunch. They also note the lack of a variety of fresh fruits or vegetables. They realize that they could bring their lunch daily but believe that the hospital should set an example. Furthermore, the availability of more varied and healthier choices would raise morale. Keep in mind that the cafeteria menu is basically the same as the patient menu with one special daily.

A. Who would be the likely administrative person asked to look into the complaint and implement changes if necessary/possible? Why?

B. You are an intern working at the facility. The administrator designated to follow up has asked you to assess the complaint and submit a report. Review all appropriate material in the manual and do the following:
   1) Document the validity of the complaints: Identify positive and problem aspects of menu choices.
   2) Identify changes you would recommend (if any). If you do not recommend changes, explain your rationale in detail (for example, not needed and why; inadequate staffing and why; inadequate budget, resources, too many possible barriers to overcome, etc).
   3) Identify the specific impact of the suggested changes on relevant dietary department units, staffing, and budget.
   4) Identify other administrative and/or supervisory staff who would need to be involved to effect changes. Identify nonsupervisory staff who would be involved in effecting changes. How should the administrator assigned to follow up approach these groups? Who would be directly responsible for seeing that changes are made?
   5) What possible problems/obstacles/attitudes may be presented by the supervisory and nonsupervisory staff that could impede or make change difficult ?

C. What are the pros and cons of serving the same basic menu to patients and to staff in the cafeteria except for specialty items in the cafeteria?

21. Select one day of the menu cycle for patients and modify the menu for a given therapeutic diet. Use a diet manual in making your changes. Try to avoid making unnecessary changes so labor costs and inventory are not unnecessarily increased.

22. The hospital administration is considering converting to "room service" in the next year. This type of service would closely resemble hotel room service and would essentially allow patients to call down to the foodservice department switchboard and order food whenever they were hungry. The administrator says he heard about this innovative foodservice concept at a national Hospital Association convention. Put together a preliminary report outlining the changes necessary in the current operation and the benefits and possible obstacles and concerns with such a service. How will the budget and weekly operating report be affected by such a change? In other words, what expenses would go up and what expenses would decline?

GROUP ACTIVITIES

Many decisions in foodservice are made by a team. The following activities are designed to be completed in groups, with input from all team/group members. Evaluation of team members is an important component of this process. The form on page 40 can be used for this purpose. It will allow you to practice skills in constructive criticism. Use a separate page for each group member. Be sure to make copies of the evaluation form before filling it out.

Marketing Project (Inlet Isles Case Study Problem 5)

The purpose of this assignment is to develop a marketing plan to increase revenue for the Department of Food and Nutrition Services of Inlet Isles Medical Center.

This assignment has both a written and an oral component. For the written report, use problem 5 of the case study (see page 32). Answer parts A and B. Also answer part C as far as estimating weekly and yearly revenue and adjusting the budget. It is not necessary to adjust the weekly operating report, determine the effects on cost per patient day, or do part D. Also include a written summary of your marketing plan.

Each group will also give an oral presentation. The point is to convince the hospital board (the others in the class) that your marketing plan is feasible and will generate revenue. You should be prepared to answer questions from the board. It is recommended that you use visual aids to enhance your presentation.

Students will work in groups of three and will receive a group grade. All members of the group should participate in both the written and oral parts of the assignment.

Case Scenarios Assignment

For this assignment, students will present and discuss the scenarios from the Inlet Isles case study. Students will work in groups of three. Each group will present two case studies. Each member of the group should participate in the planning and in the presentation, and a group grade will be given.

The lead group should:

Present the scenario and identify the problem(s).
Lead a discussion of concerns and possible solutions.
Compile a list of the suggested solutions.
Attempt to have the class reach a consensus about which solutions would be mostworkable.

Each scenario can lead to considerable discussion. The group presenting the scenario is responsible for leading a discussion that involves all class members and covers a wide variety of possible concerns and solutions. *All students need to read all the scenarios and should be prepared to discuss them.*

Confidential Evaluation of Team Member Contributions

Evaluation for: _____

Please answer the following questions regarding the contributions of this individual to the team project using the following scale:

1 = did not meet expectations   2 = met expectations   3 = exceeded expectations

	Scale		
Attended all/most team planning and work meetings	1	2	3
Actively contributed during team meetings	1	2	3
Willingly took on tasks to complete for each meeting	1	2	3
Open-minded toward others' ideas	1	2	3
Willing and able to compromise within the team	1	2	3
Contributed his or her fair share toward completion of the project	1	2	3

Positive comments regarding this person's ability to work as part of a team toward a common goal:

Suggestions for improvement of this person's ability to work as part of a team (please use constructive comments):

Other comments:

Team member submitting evaluation: _____

SPREADSHEET EXERCISES

Spreadsheet Scenarios

These scenarios allow you to make some changes to the weekly operating report (WOR) for week 10 and observe how this affects total expenses, total revenues, and net expenses. In order to protect the original spreadsheet, **it is advisable to copy the WOR to the hard drive or another disk before beginning.** Note that the letter/number pairs in parentheses refer to the cell location on the spreadsheet.

Scenario One—Decreasing Food Costs

Pull up the original Weekly Operating Report file (file name: WOR) from your hard drive or disk.

Before making any changes in the spreadsheet, copy down the following numbers from the original weekly operating report:

Food cost (I8) _____

Total expenses (B94) _____

Total revenue (B95) _____

Cost per patient day (D96)_____

Year-to-date cost per patient day (D101) _____

Now change the following numbers for food purchases in the spreadsheet:

Change meat purchases to $3500 (B4)

Change dairy purchases to $1350 (C4)

Change bakery purchases to $1100 (D4)

Change grocery purchases to $4300 (F4)

What is the new food cost (I8)? _____

How much was saved compared to the original food cost? _____

How much are the new total expenses (B94)? _____

How much did this change compared to the original amount? _____

How much is the new total revenue (B95)? _____

How much did this change compared to the original amount? _____

What is the new cost per patient day (D96)? _____

How did this change compared to the original amount?_____

What is the year-to-date cost per patient day (D101)? _____

How did this change compared to the original amount? _____

Do these new values for cost per patient day (PPD) and cost PPD year to date (YTD) meet the budgeted amounts (G96 and 101)? _____

Give some examples of ways to decrease food costs using the Inlet Isles menus.

You may print the spreadsheet and/or save as a new file entitled WOR_S1. Before proceeding to Scenario 2, exit this revised spreadsheet and pull up the original Weekly Operating Report (WOR) File.

Notes

Scenario Two: Decreasing Labor Costs

Pull up the original Weekly Operating Report file (file name:WOR) from your hard drive or disk.

Before making any changes in the spreadsheet, copy down the following numbers from the weekly operating report:

Total expenses (B94) _____

Total revenue (B95) _____

Cost per patient day (D96) _____

Year-to-date cost per patient day (D101) _____

Now change the total labor costs in the spreadsheet:

Change labor to $27,000 (B79)

How much are the new total expenses (B94)? _____

How did this change compared to the original amount? _____

How much is the new total revenue (B95)? _____

How much did this change compared to the original amount? _____

What is the new cost per patient day (D96)? _____

How much did this change compared to the original amount? _____

What is the new year-to-date cost per patient day (D101)? _____

How much did this change compared to the original amount? _____

Do these new values for cost per patient day (PPD) and cost PPD year to date (YTD) meet the budgeted amounts (G96 and 101)? _____

Give some examples of how labor costs could be decreased at Inlet Isles.

You may print the spreadsheet and/or save as a new file entitled WOR_S2. Before proceeding to Scenario 3, exit this revised spreadsheet and pull up the original Weekly Operating Report (WOR) File.

Notes

Scenario Three: Increasing Revenues

Pull up the original Weekly Operating Report file (file name:WOR) from your hard drive or disk.

Before making any changes in the spreadsheet, copy down the following numbers from the weekly operating report:

      Subtotal cash sales (F30) _____

      Total revenue (B95) _____

      Cost per patient day (D96) _____

      Year-to-date cost per patient day (D101) _____

Now change cafeteria sales to $13,000 (F25) in the spreadsheet.

What is the new subtotal cash sales (F30)? _____

How much did this change compared to the original amount? _____

What is the new amount for cash sales (B69)? _____

How is this related to the subtotal for cash sales (F30)? _____

What is the new total revenue (B95)? _____

How much did this change compared to the original amount? _____

What is the new cost per patient day (D96)? _____

How much did this change compared to the original amount?_____

What is the new year-to-date cost per patient day (D101)? _____

How much did this change compared to the original amount? _____

Do these new values for cost per patient day (PPD) and cost PPD year to date (YTD) meet the budgeted amounts (G 96 and 101)? _____

What are some strategies for increasing cafeteria sales at Inlet Isles?

You may print the spreadsheet and/or save as a new file entitled WOR_S3. Before proceeding to Scenario 4, exit this revised spreadsheet and pull up the original Weekly Operating Report (WOR) File.

Notes

Scenario Four: Decreasing Revenues

Pull up the original Weekly Operating Report file (file name: WOR) from your hard drive or disk.

Before making any changes in the spreadsheet, copy down the following numbers from the weekly operating report:

        Total revenue (B95) _____

        Cost per patient day (D96) _____

        Year-to-date cost per patient day (D101) _____

Eliminate charges for floor stocks (F21), nourishments (F22), tubefeedings (F23), and outpatient counseling (F29).

What is the new total revenue (B95)? _____

How much did this change compared to the original amount? _____

What is the new cost per patient day (D96)? _____

How much did this change compared to the original amount? _____

What is the new year-to-date cost per patient day (D101)? _____

How much did this change compared to the original amount? _____

Do these new values for cost per patient day (PPD) and cost PPD year to date (YTD) meet the budgeted amounts (G96 and 101)? _____

Do you recommend eliminating these charges at Inlet Isles?

You may print the spreadsheet and/or save as a new file entitled WOR_S4.

Scenario Five

Combine any two of the scenarios above. Determine whether the cost per patient day and the year-to-date cost per patient day meet the budgeted amounts.

Notes

Notes